362.82   T 63300 $17.96
MOO
   MOORE-MALLINOS, JENNIFER
   LOST AND FOUND

DATE DUE

NOV 1 5 2007			

HIGHSMITH 45230

This book
belongs to:

....

....

Lost
and Found

Text: *Jennifer Moore-Mallinos*

Illustrations: *Marta Fàbrega*

BARRON'S

"One of my jobs of being your big sister is to teach you all the things that I've already learned. When I was about your age, Mom and Dad took me to the fair in town. I'll never forget that day because that's the day that I learned that getting lost was no fun at all, it was scary!"

"What happened?"

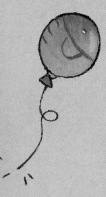

"It was a hot summer day and we were all excited to be at the fair. There were people everywhere. The whole town must have been there because no matter which way we turned there were people all around us!"

"We had just arrived at the fair and as usual, Mom was holding on tightly to my hand. Dad walked ahead of us so he could clear a path through the crowd. Just as we were walking through a large group of people, I saw that my shoelace was untied. Without even thinking, I pulled my hand away from Mom's tight grasp and bent down to tie my shoe, but when I stood up Mom was gone!"

8-9

"There I stood, all alone, while crowds of strangers weaved around me..."

"I yelled so loud my throat hurt, but Mom and Dad couldn't hear me. I was lost! My eyes filled with tears and I started to get really scared, I didn't know what to do. Should I walk around and try to find Mom and Dad or should I wait to see if they come back? Just then, out of the crowd popped a police officer. He must have known that I was lost because he came right over to me and asked if I needed help. I cried and said YES."

"I knew he was a police officer because he was dressed in a dark blue uniform and had a special badge on the front of his shirt. When he knelt down to wipe my tears, he smiled and told me that everything was going to be all right. He said he was going to help me find Mom and Dad, but first he needed to ask me a few questions."

"First he asked me what my name was, and if I knew my address and telephone number. Then he asked me what Mom and Dad looked like and

what they were wearing. When he asked me if I knew Mom or Dad's cell phone number, and I didn't know it, I started to cry. I was scared that I would be lost forever! That's when I learned how important it was for me to know Mom and Dad's cell phone number."

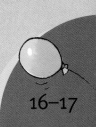

"Then the police officer explained that he needed to take me to a special place called the LOST AND FOUND, where kids who were lost go to find their parents. He took my hand, and we started to make our way through the crowd. I remember I was so scared that I squeezed his hand as tight as I could, so I wouldn't get lost again!"

"When we arrived at the LOST AND FOUND, there were lots of other kids already there. Some of the kids were sitting quietly with tears streaming down their faces, while others were crying hard and screaming for their parents. That's when I started to panic that Mom and Dad wouldn't find me. I worried about how scared and upset they must have been when they realized that I was lost."

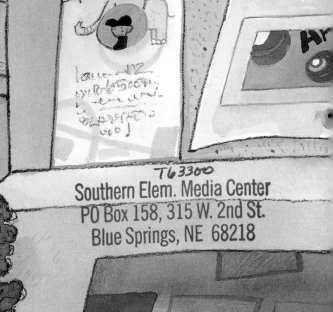

T63300

Southern Elem. Media Center
PO Box 158, 315 W. 2nd St.
Blue Springs, NE 68218

"Why didn't you tell the police officer about your meeting place? Mom and Dad would have been looking for you there."

"We never thought to have a meeting place before this happened! But now we all know that no matter where we go, we always have a meeting place picked out, just in case one of us gets lost!"

"It seemed like I sat at the LOST and FOUND forever, but after a while the police officer, who was now my friend, came over to see how I was doing.

He handed me a fuzzy panda bear, put his hand on my shoulder, and told me that everything was going to be all right. I tried to be brave and not cry, but it didn't work."

"What happened when Mom and Dad found you?"

"I'll never forget how happy I was when I saw them rush through the door! They ran over to me, swooped me up into their arms, and we all cried."

"Even Dad?"

"Even Dad! When we left to go back into the fair, I remember walking by the other kids and thinking how lucky I was that Mom and Dad found me. I also thought that those kids should calm down, because it was just a matter of time before their parents would arrive."

"Now, whenever I see your panda bear, I'll never forget how scary it was when you were lost, even for Mom and Dad! I guess holding Mom or Dad's hand and having a meeting place, no matter where we go, isn't such a bad idea after all!"

"And don't forget to learn Mom and Dad's cell phone numbers too!"

"I'm glad you were found and I'm glad you're my big sister. You're the best!"

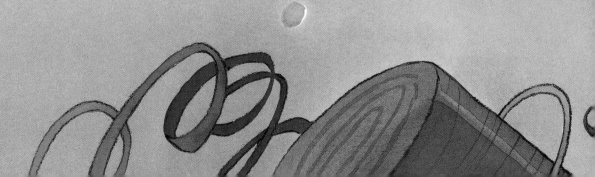

guidelines
to parents

As parents we constantly worry about the safety of our children. Making sure that our children don't wander off and get lost is just one of the many worries we have as parents. As terrifying as the thought may be, it's something we need to think about and discuss with our children.

The feeling of panic parents feel when they realize that their child has wandered off and is lost is unbearable. What would you do? What would your child do? Would they know whom to ask for help? Do they know their full name, telephone number, and address? As parents it's our job to make sure we provide our children with the necessary tools to assist them in maintaining their own safety.

Lost and Found highlights the terrifying fact that sometimes, despite our efforts, children wander off and get lost. This book can be used as a tool to facilitate and stimulate discussion between you and your child regarding his or her safety. You and your children will have the opportunity to explore various strategies that may lessen their chance of becoming lost, and to develop their skills to recall relevant information if they get lost.

It is imperative for every child to know their full name, home address, and home telephone number, as well as the number for each parent's cell phone. For some children, having to learn such information may seem overwhelming and may be difficult for them to remember. Therefore it's up to us to make learning this information fun and not scary. Don't forget, kids thrive on repetition, silly songs, and simple rhymes.

Can you describe in detail exactly what your child is wearing today? Just as children need to know certain information, so do parents. Being able to describe your child in detail, as well as having a recent photo available, is essential in increasing your child's chances of being found.

Do you identify a prominent meeting place as soon as you arrive in a public place? Identifying a meeting place, such as the front entrance at the zoo or the glass elevator in the middle of the shopping mall, provides your child with an easy way to locate a focal point where you all can meet if he or she becomes lost.

As you read this book to your child, allow your enthusiasm and interest in the book's message to be heard, despite the seriousness of the topic. Children are motivated to learn when they are having fun. Therefore, the most effective way to share these concepts with your child is simply that…have fun!

LOST AND FOUND

Text: **Jennifer Moore-Mallinos**
Illustrations: **Marta Fàbrega**
Typesetting/design: **Gemser Publications, S.L.**

First edition for the United States and Canada published in 2006 by Barron's Educational Series, Inc.
Original title of the book in Spanish: *¿Te has perdido alguna vez?*
© Copyright 2006 by Gemser Publications, S.L.
El Castell, 38; Teià (08329) Barcelona, Spain (World Rights)

All inquiries should be addressed to:
Barron's Educational Series, Inc.
250 Wireless Boulevard
Hauppauge, New York 11788
http://www.barronseduc.com

ISBN-13: 978-0-7641-3510-1
ISBN-10: 0-7641-3510-4
Library of Congress Control Number 2005938259

Printed in China
9 8 7 6 5 4 3 2 1